READ THIS FIRST:

An Owner's Guide
to the New Model Statement
of Objectives for Academic
Bibliographic Instruction

Edited by
Carolyn Dusenbury
Monica Fusich
Kathleen Kenny
Beth Woodard

Bibliographic Instruction Section
Association of College & Research Libraries
American Library Association

RIT - WALLACE LIBRARY
CIRCULATING LIBRARY BOOKS

OVERDUE FINES AND FEES FOR <u>ALL</u> BORROWERS

*Recalled = $1/ day overdue (no grace period)
*Billed = $10.00/ item when returned 4 or more weeks overdue
*Lost Items = replacement cost+$10 fee
*All materials must be returned or renewed by the duedate.

READ THIS FIRST:
AN OWNER'S GUIDE TO THE NEW MODEL STATEMENT OF OBJECTIVES FOR ACADEMIC BIBLIOGRAPHIC INSTRUCTION

Editors

Carolyn Dusenbury
Monica Fusich
Kathleen Kenny
Beth Woodard

Bibliographic Instruction Section
Association of College and Research Libraries
A Division of the American Library Association
1991

Published by the Association of College and Research Libraries
A Division of the American Library Association
50 East Huron Street
Chicago, IL 60611-2795

ASSOCIATION OF
COLLEGE
& RESEARCH
LIBRARIES

ISBN: 0-8389-7548-8

This publication is printed on recyled, acid-free paper.

Printed in the United States of America.

TABLE OF CONTENTS

Introduction

Cerise Oberman
SUNY at Plattsburgh
Past Chair, ACRL BIS

In 1988 when I was elected Vice-Chair/Chair-Elect of the ACRL Bibliographic Instruction Section, the Section was completing work on what promised to become one of the most important contributions to library instruction in recent years: a revision of the almost ten year old 1979 *BIS Model Statement of Objectives and Guidelines for Bibliographic Instruction*. The task of updating the earlier *Model Statement* to reflect the current trend in library education away from tool-based instruction and toward concept-based instruction was the challenge of the Task Force on Model Statement of Objectives.[1] Appointed in 1984, the Task Force worked for three years to draft a new *Model Statement*. During this time, I had the privilege, as a BIS member-at-large, to attend many of the Task Force meetings. All of these meetings were intellectually invigorating. They were marked by substantive discussion and debate about the conceptual basis of library instruction and how to transform these concepts into a meaningful and useful document--a document which would be flexible and dynamic, rather than prescriptive and static. The Task Force finally decided to concentrate on information: how it is identified and defined, how it is structured, how it is intellectually accessed, and how it is physically organized. Thus, the Task Force believed it was ensuring that the new *Model Statement* would achieve its goal of being firmly rooted in concepts. Furthermore, with emphasis on information concepts, the *Model Statement* would be able to transcend technological changes, pedagogical styles, and institutionally specific concerns.

In early 1987, a draft of the *Model Statement of Objectives for Academic Bibliographic Instruction* was completed and published in a Spring issue of *C&RL News*,[2] in part for the purpose of soliciting comments from the library community. An open hearing on the *Model Statement* followed in June at the American Library Association Annual Conference. The open hearing (at which I served as moderator) was well-attended and elicited insightful comments and useful suggestions. Perhaps the most significant (and poignant) moment, however, occurred when Lori Arp, the Chair of the Model Statement Task Force who had worked long and diligently on this project, rose and asked, "I'd like to know if people [will] really use [the *Model Statement*] or is it something that is too difficult to use?" (That was a question all of us who had been involved with the *Model Statement* had privately thought but never dared to publicly express.) There was an uneasy silence in the room. Finally, a librarian rose and replied:

> Our library is currently a very, very traditional library. We have
> not done much with technology. I particularly appreciate this
> document for being non-institution specific. I think I could very
> easily use this in my bibliographic instruction guideline that I'm
> preparing for my own staff. Additionally, I think this will be very
> helpful for me to take to other committees on campus such as the
> curriculum committee, and in my work with other faculty members
> to convince them of the value of bibliographic instruction.[3]

Clearly, the Task Force's vision was shared by others in the academic
instructional community.

In July 1988, the *Model Statement* was accepted by ACRL as an official statement
of the Section. However, Lori Arp's question about the *Model Statement*'s
usability and accessibility continued to haunt me. It seemed to me that while
ACRL acceptance of the *Model Statement* marked the official completion of the
document, it also signaled the beginning of another important task--ensuring that
the *Model Statement* was truly accessible to instruction librarians. From my
perspective, the document was too important merely to be "adopted" as official
dogma; it needed to be understood and actively applied in the field. Therefore,
the *Model Statement* became the focus of my tenure as BIS Vice-Chair/Chair-
Elect.

To assist me in this, I appointed a Task Force on Access to the Model
Statement.[4] The charge to the Task Force was to develop a set of
recommendations for bringing the document to the attention of the library
instruction community and to recommend ways in which BIS could facilitate the
practical and pragmatic application of this conceptual document. The Task Force
worked closely with the 1990 Conference Program Planning Committee[5] which
chose the *Model Statement* as the focus of the annual BIS program. This
publication is a result of the combined work of the Task Force and the Conference
Program Planning Committee.

The 1990 BIS Conference Program was designed to provide broad exposure to the
new *Model Statement*. "Read This First: An Owner's Guide to the BIS Model
Statement" recognized that the new *Model Statement* was a dramatic departure
from the 1979 *Model Statement*. Therefore, it was imperative that the program
not only make librarians aware of the existence of this new document, but also
provide assistance in understanding the background, content, and potential uses
of the document. As such, the program was designed around three questions:
What is the purpose of this new *Model Statement*? What is the content of the

Model Statement? How can it be used in designing instructional programs? The three papers and four poster sessions presented at the program (and contained in this volume) have begun the process of answering these questions.

Mary Ellen Litzinger's "The Model Statement of Objectives: An Analysis" is an excellent general review of the purpose and content of the *Model Statement*. Litzinger asks the hard questions: What is the *Model Statement*? What does it say? How do we use it? Her overview examines and explains the terminology in the document, as well as the document's structure. Most importantly, Litzinger addresses the importance of the document in designing instructional programs. Effectively, this paper is a road map for instruction librarians to begin exploring the *Model Statement*.

Carol Wright, in her paper "Application of the Model Statement to a Basic Information Access Skills Program at Penn State University" explains the development of a basic information access skills program which used the *Model Statement* as its foundation. Of particular interest is the way in which the program at Penn State relied on examining the concepts of the *Model Statement* in the context of learning theory. The result is an Information Access Skills Matrix combining concepts with learning levels.

At the University of Colorado at Denver, Rutherford Witthus has applied the *Model Statement* to a non-traditional instructional program. In "Understanding the Present in the Past: Instruction in the Use of Original Source Materials," Witthus provides insight into one way the *Model Statement* was used as a basis for developing objectives for a unique instructional program using archival materials. By using the *Model Statement* as a guide, Witthus redrafted the *Model Statement*'s terminal objectives to reflect concepts unique to archival research. His thinking illustrates both the flexibility and the universality of the *Model Statement* in supporting instructional programs.

The four poster sessions presented at the Conference displayed four unique interpretations and applications of the *Model Statement* to functioning library instruction programs. The diversity of programs and institutions using the *Model Statement* is yet another indication that the *Model Statement* can be used effectively in a variety of settings.

The publication of the proceedings of the 1990 BIS Program brings a sense of closure to my personal involvement with the *Model Statement*. It also brings a sense of great satisfaction. More importantly, taken together, these three papers provide instruction librarians with multiple perspectives on the significance of the new *Model Statement*. Hopefully, these papers can serve as a collective springboard for examining, exploring, and adapting the *Model Statement* as a foundation for all academic instructional programs.

Notes

1. ACRL BIS Task Force on Model Statement of Objectives. Committee members: Lori Arp (chair), Barbara Beaton, Joseph Boisse, Julie Czisny, David Ginn, Roland Person, Jan Rice, and Beth Woodard.

2. *College & Research Libraries News*, Mary 1987, pp. 256-261.

3. Diana Gonzalez (Antelope Valley College), statement during the ACRL BIS Open Hearing on the Model Statement, San Francisco, California, 29 June 1987.

4. ACRL BIS Task Force on Access to the Model Statement. Committee members: Mary Ellen Larson Litzinger (chair, 1989-1990), Carolyn Dusenbury, Monica Fusich (chair, 1990-1991), Kathleen Kenny, Beth Woodard, Andrea Wyman, and Lori Arp (ex-officio).

5. ACRL BIS 1990 Conference Program Planning Committee. Committee members: Susan Hoffman (chair), Shirley Black, Debra Costa, Michael Miranda, Loanne Snavely, and Red Wassenich.

Model Statement Of Objectives For Academic Bibliographic Instruction

ACRL Bibliographic Instruction Section

The primary purpose of the Model Statement is to generate thinking in the discipline of bibliographic instruction concerning the direction of existing instructional programs. It is intended to help librarians articulate and focus on what their instructional objectives should be and stimulate research into whether existing programs are achieving these objectives. As such, the Statement is not designed to introduce the new librarian to the field, nor is it designed to introduce an outside faculty member to the relevant concepts within the discipline. Rather, it is intended to serve as a statement of general direction for practicing librarians to review when examining current instructional programs or developing the keystones of new programs.

The role of bibliographic instruction is not only to provide students with the specific skills needed to complete assignments, but to prepare individuals to make effective life-long use of information, information sources, and information systems. To this end, the Model Statement attempts to outline the pertinent processes individuals use when gathering information. The Statement does not attempt to be comprehensive. The content is designed as a set of examples or points of departure and is not intended to serve as an institution's primary document.

The Model Statement is comprised of a set of general and terminal objectives which describe the general processes used when gathering information. Three objectives are normally used to describe the learning activities desired for a particular instructional unit. These objectives describe the overall goals of the programs and what the program is intended to achieve. Terminal objectives break down the overall objectives into specific discrete measurable results. Enabling (behavioral) objectives define the specific knowledge or skills necessary to achieve the terminal objectives. They are associated with the behavior of the person who has to master the material. Since each institution must determine their own enabling objectives, they are not included in this document, which attempts to generalize the processes used to access information.

For convenience, the series of general and terminal objectives listed in the Model Statement has been broken into four broad areas of concern with corresponding objectives listed in each of the areas. The Statement outlines how information is:

a) identified and defined by experts;

b) structured;

c) intellectually accessed;

d) physically organized and accessed.

The section headings represent significant areas or topics of concern to instruction librarians. No set order is intended.

When developing the Model Statement, the Task Force was guided by the following principles:

1. User groups targeted by the objectives. The Model Statement is designed to address the needs of all potential user groups within academic libraries. This was done for two reasons: 1) Experience has shown that there is no homogeneous group of "students" or even "undergraduates," but rather there exists a diverse student body whose members operate on a continuum of research sophistication; 2) Increasing sophistication in the field of bibliographic instruction has resulted in the development of many excellent programs of instruction for student, faculty and university staff alike. The revised document attempts to reflect the needs of these user groups also.

2. Ordering of the objectives. Depending on the information need of the individual or group in question, the librarian may find instruction in "highly sophisticated" information skills essential for the undergraduate, while the graduate student or even the faculty member may need training in basic skills. In order to provide the greatest flexibility, the objectives are not ordered; rather, it is for the librarian to determine what objectives fulfill the needs of the specific user group in question.

3. Institution- and tool-specific information. It would be literally impossible to list all the objectives which describe institutional and tool- specific differences. The Model Statement reviews the similarities within these sources and focuses on the process of using information and information sources, recorded and unrecorded, rather than focusing on library processes. The document is therefore conceptually based and does not include tool-specific or institution-specific detail. The Task Force feels that tool-specific or institution-specific information is more appropriately placed within enabling objectives.

4. Language used. The Model Statement uses very specific language to describe generic processes. Since common terms used by librarians have different and often divergent meanings, it is recommended that the attached glossary be consulted when using the document.

5. Incorporation of technological advances. Advances in technology have been incorporated into various sections of the document where appropriate rather than examined separately. For example, the methods used to retrieve information sources from an online catalog are explained in the "Intellectually Accessed" section, and the explanation that a catalog is a holding list is detailed in the "Physically Organized and Accessed" section. By describing processes rather than tools, it is hoped that the Statement will remain effective long after the present "new" technology becomes old.

6. Evaluation of information sources and systems. It was felt that evaluation of information, information sources, and information systems is something that occurs throughout the search process. To this end, evaluation issues have been incorporated into each section of the document where appropriate.

7. Evaluation of objectives. Specific attention was not devoted to developing evaluation designs for the attainment of objectives in an instructional setting, as it was felt that guidance in this matter was available through *Evaluating Bibliographic Instruction: A Handbook*, published by ACRL's Bibliographic Instruction Section in 1983.

8. Structural flexibility. The structure of the document has been designed to permit as much flexibility as possible. It consists of four major areas of concern, each with its own general and terminal objectives. It is probable that no one library's program will include all the objectives listed; rather, each objective is suggested as an element related to the area of concern. The flexibility of the document lies in its "mix and match" nature; terminal objectives of one section may be matched with terminal objectives of another section depending upon the program being designed. In addition, the Model Statement simply lists suggested areas of interest; when designing a program, the librarian may find that additional terminal objectives must be created in order to reflect the needs of the group in question.

Using the Model Statement

The Model Statement is designed to be used in two ways. First, it is intended to serve as a checklist through which to assist and examine present programs. Second, it is intended to serve as a resource through which to develop new programs. To use the Statement effectively for the latter purpose, the following steps are recommended:

1. Define the user group and the present level of sophistication;
2. Determine the purpose of instruction;

3.   Determine which overall sections of the document are relevant to the proposed program;

4.   Select the relevant terminal objectives from each section;

5.   If needed, create additional subpoints to the terminal objectives selected;

6.   Develop enabling objectives.

Model Statement of General and Terminal Objectives

1.   How information is identified and defined by experts.

General Objective: The user understands how information is defined by experts, and recognizes how that knowledge can help determine the direction of his/her search for specific information.

T1*. The user understands that individuals or groups identify themselves as belonging to specific areas and/or disciplines.

T2. The user recognizes that individuals within these groups may combine information from information sources with original thought, experimentation, and/or analysis to produce new information.

T3.   The user recognizes that disciplines use specific methods to communicate information.
a.   The user recognizes that information sources can be recorded or unrecorded sources which may appear in different physical formats.
b.   The user recognizes that information sources go through various review processes to be accepted as credible by the research community.
c. The user understands the processes through which information sources are accepted and disseminated in the research community.

T4.   Once a topic of interest is selected, the user understands how it can be refined and can formulate a question.
a.   The user recognizes when a question is discipline-specific or interdisciplinary.
b.   The user understands that the initial question may be too broad or narrow to investigate effectively and that adjustment in scope, direction, or timeframe may be needed.

T5.   The user understands how to construct an approach or strategy appropriate to the anticipated result of the research process.

a. The user understands that the identification of specific information sources will depend on the individual question and the strategy devised.

b. The user recognizes that the audience of the end product will in part determine the direction and type of search conducted.

c. The user understands that the form and the purpose of the end product will in part determine the direction and type of search conducted.

2. How information sources are structured.

General Objective: The user understands the importance of the organizational content, bibliographic structure, function, and use of information sources.

T1. The user understands how the organizational content of recorded information sources is structured and how this knowledge can help determin the usefulness of the source.

a. The user understands the importance of evaluating the author's credentials.

b. The user understands how the timeliness or the date of publication may determine the value of a source.

c. The user recognizes that the publisher's reputation may affect the usefulness of the source. The user recognizes that in periodical publications, the editorial review process is as important as the publishing information.

d. The user recognizes the importance of title, thesis, preface, introduction, table of contents, appendixes, summary, and/or abstract in evaluating the scope, limitations, and special features of the information source and thereby its usefulness.

e. The user recognizes that the purpose of the author in presenting ideas, opinions, or research may in part determine the usefulness of the source.

f. The user recognizes the organization or arrangement of an information source may affect its value (hierarchical, alphabetical, chronological, tabular, regional, classified, schematic, or numerical).

g. The user recognizes that the amount and type of documentation used may affect the value of a recorded information source.

T2. The user recognizes that unrecorded information sources exist and can evaluate their potential usefulness.

a. The user recognizes the importance of the individual's or group's credentials and is able to evaluate this information to determine the source's credibility in relation to the topic.

b. The user recognizes the importance of evaluating the timeliness of the information.

c.   The user recognizes the importance of correctly identifying the source's thesis and arguments to determine whether the information provided is pertinent to the topic.

T3.   The user understands how information sources are bibliographically structured and how this knowledge can help determine the usefulness of the source.
a.   The user recognizes that the information needed to identify information sources is manipulated into systematic sequences called citations and that the amount of information required and the form of a citation may vary from field to field.
a.1.   The user recognizes that the bibliographic structure of recorded information sources may vary among disciplines and within subject areas.
a.2.   The user recognizes the major types of citations and knows where they typically occur (documentary notes, in-text citations, bibliographic entries, etc.).
a.3.   The user recognizes that the form of a citation varies for different subject areas and disciplines.
a.4.   The user recognizes that the amount of information required in a citation varies for different subject areas and disciplines.
b.   The user understands the relationship of citations to other information sources.
b.1.   The user understands that the purpose of a citation is to enable others to identify and locate pertinent information sources.
b.2.   The user understands that some sources may indirectly refer to other sources through the use of incomplete citations (implicit vs. explicit footnotes).
b.3.   The user understands the significance of identifying information sources which are repeatedly cited by more than one source.
b.4.   The user understands the link between the information provided within a citation and the organizational structure of the source cited and recognizes the importance of the link in evaluating the usefulness of the source identified.

3.   How information sources are intellectually accessed by users.

General Objective: The user can identify useful information from information sources or information systems.

T1.   The user understands that although any information about an information source could be used to help identify and locate it, there are certain elements of information called access points which are accepted by the research community as the most pertinent through which to identify a source.

a. The user recognizes that the "author" entry is a commonly used access point.

b. The user recognizes that the title of a recorded information source is another commonly used access point.

c. The user recognizes that a "subject," topic, or description field is a commonly used access point.

d. The user recognizes that the use of additional access points depends on the structure and format of the source used to identify new information.

d.1. The user recognizes that each element of information found within a citation may potentially be used as an access point.

d.2. The user recognizes that information found within an abstract or summary may potentially be used as an access point (usually through the method of key word searching where each word can be used as an access point).

d.3. The user recognizes that additional access may be available through codes, categories, or mapping which may not be obvious in the information source or system.

e. The user understands that some sources use controlled vocabulary assigned by an indexer, cataloger, or computer programmer as access points.

e.1. The user recognizes that most controlled vocabulary describes the subject or author of the information source.

e.2. The user recognizes that the rules governing indexing practices may influence the process of retrieval.

e.3. The user understands that there may be printed or online lists or thesauri which may aid in the identification of these access points.

e.4. The user recognizes the relationship of broader, narrower, and related terms.

T2. The user understands that there are a variety of information sources called access tools whose primary purpose is to identify other information sources through the use of access points.

a. The user recognizes that access tools used vary by discipline or subject area.

b. The user recognizes that access tools used vary by the type of information source needed.

c. The user recognizes that access tools vary in format and recognizes the implications of format as it relates to the availability of access points.

d. The user recognizes the importance of the organizational content of the access tools in determining whether or not it is a good information source.

e. The user understands that no access tool is comprehensive in scope.

f. The user understands the importance of selecting the appropriate access tool in order to identify useful information sources.

T3. The user understands how to manipulate access points to identify useful information or information sources.

a. The user understands when it is appropriate to search for information through the use of a single access point.

b. The user understands the concept of Boolean logic and its importance in searching for information under more than one access point.

c. The user understands the importance of browsing.

d. The user understands the importance of proximity searching (looking for two or more words in the same sentence, paragraph, record or file).

e. The user understands that given insufficient information to identify a particular access point, there are steps which may help identify it.

e.1. The user understands truncation.

e.2. The user understands key word searching and knows when it may be appropriate and possible.

T4. The user can evaluate the citation retrieved or the information accessed and determine whether or not it is at the appropriate level of specificity.

T5. The user recognizes the absence of recorded information sources on a specific topic, realizes the implications and recognizes the alternatives.

a. The user realizes that the lack of recorded information sources does not preclude the existence of unrecorded information sources.

b. The user recognizes that the lack of recorded information may suggest the necessity of original analysis or data collection.

c. The user recognizes that he/she may have to change the direction of the search if the use of unrecorded information sources or the gathering of primary data is not feasible.

4. How information sources are physically organized and accessed.

General Objective: The user understands the way collections of information sources are physically organized and accessed.

T1. The user understands that libraries and library systems may group information sources by subject, author, format, publisher, type of material, or special audience.

a. The user recognizes that may library systems are decentralized and the materials at each location may be distinguished by subject, format, publisher, type of material, or by special audience.

b. The user recognizes that materials in like formats are usually housed together in special areas of the library or in particular units of the library system along with the appropriate equipment needed to utilize these materials.

c. The user understands that a library may choose to house materials by one publisher together in one location or disperse them throughout the library's holdings.

d. The user recognizes that types of materials may be grouped together in order to provide ease of use or because of preservation and maintenance concerns.

e. The user recognizes that some libraries provide separate collections for special user groups.

f. The user understands that materials on like subjects may be designated by the subject area or discipline.

f.1. The user recognizes that some branches of a library system may be designated by the subject area or discipline.

f.2. The user understands that classification schemes are designed to enable libraries to locate materials on the same subject in the same discipline in close proximity to each other.

T2. The user understands that the library uses call numbers to assign a unique physical address to each item in the collection.

T3. The user understands that individual items within a library system's collections are listed in special holdings or location files.

a. The user understands that there is usually a central holdings or location file for the library's collection and that it might be in one or more formats.

b. The user understands that various special collections in the library or library system may have special holdings files and that they may or may not be subsets of the central file.

c. The user is aware that there are special files which can be used to identify the holdings of items available from other libraries.

T4. The user understands that the library staff is comprised of individuals with varying degrees and areas of expertise, who provide certain services through departments and who may be helpful in accessing information.

T5. The user understands the policies and procedures used by library departments and recognizes that these may vary.

T6. The user understands that the campus library is not the only location through which to retrieve necessary material.

a. The user recognizes that libraries do not have comprehensive holdings and that one library may lend an item from its collection, or furnish a copy of an item from its collection to another library not under the same administration.

b. The user recognizes that in order to facilitate library cooperation in resource sharing, may libraries have developed networks and consortia.

c. The user understands that information sources may be available for purchase by individuals through publishers and or document delivery services and that some information sources are only available on a purchase basis.

d. The user recognizes that personal networks may be essential to retrieving appropriate information.

GLOSSARY

Access: to retrieve information.

Access points: specific pieces of information identified as being useful to the retrieval of information.

Bibliographic structure: the framework of explicit links of footnote references and bibliographic citations or implicit links of tacit relationships.

Citation: a bibliographic record (or systematic sequence) which includes the information necessary to access an information source physically.

Communication: the transfer of information in the various media from one person, place, or device to another.

Data: the symbols or characters of a language. Examples: the letter of the alphabet, numbers, etc.

Document (Recorded Information Source): a physical entity in any medium upon which is recorded all or part of a work or multiple works. Examples: book journal article, etc.

Information: a grouping of data which has a particular meaning within a specific context.
Examples: a word, a name, etc.

Information source: a single entity from which information is retrieved.
Examples: a person, a book, a journal article, an index, etc.

Information system: an organized structure of interrelated information sources.
Examples: an online catalog, etc.

Intellectual access: the isolation or selecting of useful information from information sources or systems.

Physical access: the physical retrieval of an information source.

Process: manipulating, preparing, and handling information to achieve the desired results.

Structure: the logical arrangement or organization of information.

Unrecorded information: oral communication.

The Model Statement of Objectives: An Analysis

Mary Ellen Litzinger
The Pennsylvania State University

A sentiment which consoles librarians in these troubled budgetary times was first voiced by Thomas Carlyle over a century ago: "A true university is a collection of books." It is the fond hope of those in academic libraries that a well-filled library, accompanied by a state-of-the-art information access system, will bestow intellectual prestige on an institution and signal to the world that "here is a place of serious scholarship." But just as providing a population with pencils does not guarantee their ability to write, providing library users with books and other information materials does not mean that they can find information. It is the process of information gathering and utilization that ensures that users will leave the library more empowered than when they entered. The *Model Statement of Objectives* describes a process-oriented approach to designing user education programs that teaches users how to select and evaluate information as well as manipulate information sources. To understand what the *Model Statement* hopes to accomplish, it's useful to focus such an analysis around three questions: "What is the *Model Statement*?", "What does it say?" and "How is it used?".

What is the Model Statement?

The goal of the *Model Statement* is NOT to be a comprehensive curriculum plan. Rather, its primary purpose is to generate thinking about the direction of existing programs. It doesn't present a "cookbook" approach to bibliographic instruction, but a paradigm or model of a process that can be generalized to many programs. In short, the statement seeks to stimulate rather than prescribe.

The focus of this paradigm is the activity of "information gathering," which the *Model Statement* outlines as four separate but interactive processes:

1) **Information Recognition**, the process of identifying how information is created and communicated;
2) **Information Structure**, the organization of information into recorded and unrecorded sources;
3) **Information Access**, the selection of information using a number of access points and sources; and
4) **Physical Access**, the actual retrieval of an item from a collection.

These processes, which are analyzed in greater detail below, are the four programmatic units that form the structural basis of the *Model Statement*.

Underlying the document is a philosophy that bibliographic instruction is more than an education in learning how to use information sources. It should provide a cognitive framework that guides the lifelong use of information. Viewed in this light, the useful library assignment is not one that teaches how to use *Business Periodicals Index*, but one that demonstrates why and when this source should be used and generalizes this knowledge to other subject indexes as well.

Given the recent focus on information literacy, it is logical to wonder what distinguishes the *Model Statement* from its sister documents like the *Report of the Presidential Commission on Information Literacy*. While publications such as the *Report* are intended for librarians in all facets of the profession, the *Model Statement* is best suited for librarians who have some experience with bibliographic instruction programs. It should not be used as a "stand-alone" representation of an individual program. It's most appropriate use in that arena would be as a touchstone to reflect current thinking about a locally established program. Nor should it be used as the primary introduction to bibliographic instruction; a new version of the *Bibliographic Instruction Handbook*, entitled *Learning to Teach*, is currently in preparation by the Bibliographic Instruction Section. This publication, and its companion volume, *Sourcebook for Bibliographic Instruction* (also forthcoming from the Bibliographic Instruction Section), would be more appropriate for this task. The *Model Statement's* intended audience is the practicing librarian who wants to review an existing program and use the *Model Statement's* program objectives as keystones to guide the development of a new curriculum.

What does it say?

To understand the answer to the question "What does it say?", it might be helpful to explain some the important terms that are used throughout the document. These terms encompass two areas of emphasis: information and access.

Three terms are used hierarchically to describe the concept of "information":

1) **"Information"** is the smallest unit of the hierarchy and it consists of a grouping of data which has a particular meaning in a specific context (for example, a title, a name, a publisher);

2) An **"information source"** is a single entity from which information is retrieved (for example, a person, a book, an index);

3) An **"information system"** is an organized structure of interrelated information sources (an online catalog, for example).

Even though these words may be used interchangeably in other documents, each term has a unique meaning in the *Model Statement*. Two terms are used to describe the concept of "access". Their difference may appear slight at first glance, but it is substantial on further examination: 1) **"intellectual access"** refers to the selection and evaluation of interrelated information sources or systems; 2) **"physical access"** refers to the physical retrieval of the source-the "fetching" of the source and its associated processes.

In addition to understanding key terms that are used in the document, it's also helpful to understand how the document is structured. Three types of objectives are used in the *Model Statement*, two of which actually appear in the document and one whose use is implied:

1) The **"General (or Program) Objectives"** define the four primary content areas that describe the information-gathering process--information recognition, information structure, intellectual access and physical access;

2) The **"Terminal Objectives"** identify those behaviors whose achievement indicates competency in a program area. For example, one's competence in physically accessing information could be judged by how well one uses the information in a catalog to find a book or journal article in the library;

3) Not included in the *Model Statement* itself is a corresponding set of **Enabling Objectives** for each Terminal Objective. Enabling Objectives represent a specific knowledge base or set of skills that is necessary to perform the Terminal Objective .

The achievement of these Enabling Objectives is the educator's clue that he/she has done the job well. Since these sorts of behaviors are most effectively defined at a local level, where specific environments and conditions can be accounted for, they are not included in the *Model Statement*. The *Model Statement*, then, is composed of four General Objectives which deal with various phases of the information-gathering process. These objectives are each supported by several Terminal Objectives (identified as "T.1" etc. in the statement) and these objectives have several supporting objectives identified as "a," "b," and "c". This superstructure of General and Terminal objectives is supported at the local level by Enabling Objectives.

With this information in hand, it becomes easier to frame an answer to the question "What does the *Model Statement* say?". The first program area, **information**

recognition, is concerned with the question "What is information?". Its primary objective is to help the user understand how information in a particular field is defined by experts and how this definition determines the direction of an information search. The process of information recognition involves:

1) The identification of groups of scholars belonging to separate disciplines (realizing, for example, that the literature scholar will not acquire the same information patterns as a nuclear physicist);

2) A recognition that new information is created when scholars in a discipline combine existing knowledge with original thought or experimentation;

3) An understanding that each discipline communicates new information in a different way (unrecorded information may be relatively important to some fields, while published monographic and periodical information may be essential to others);

4) A realization that the processes of scholarly communication and publishing combine to affect how well an information search can be completed. The user who understands the concept of information recognition will construct a search strategy that incorporates each of the factors described above.

The objective of the information structure section is to help the user understand the importance of content organization and bibliographic communication. For example, the organizational content of a source can provide clues to its ultimate utility. The credentials of an author, his/her purposes and choice of documentary sources can signal the relative importance of a work to the informed user. Equally important to an understanding of information structure is a recognition of **bibliographic structure**. Bibliographic structure refers to the convention of listing intellectual contributions in the form of a citation. The role of citation indexes and networks in establishing subject authority is a critical concept in this area.

The third General Objective, intellectual access, encourages the user to employ an information source or system to identify useful information. This area is the strongest aspect of most bibliographic instruction programs. It includes the development of skills traditionally the province of librarians-- the manipulation of published information sources such as indexes and catalogs. The *Model Statement* expands this area to include:

1) The recognition that accepted entry points into the information system ("access points" such as subject headings and keywords) are the most efficient way to identify information;

2) The identification of appropriate "access tools," such as indexes and electronic databases, which contain these access points;

3) An understanding that the manipulation of these sources is critical to efficient information gathering. The use of Boolean logic, browsing, and proximity enhances a user's ability to effectively use an access tool.

The final General Objective, physical access, has the deceptively simple goal of helping the user to pick the source off the shelf once he/she determines its existence. The notion of physical access involves the concept that libraries group materials into several discrete collections that are sometimes determined by subject, sometimes by format and sometimes by use. Bonding these discrete collections in some sort of unity is a **"holdings or location file"**--what we would commonly think of as a catalog (although the concept isn't limited to that format). A corollary to this concept of a holdings or location file is the call number which becomes, in the terminology of the *Model Statement*, a unique form of physical address. Finally, inherent in the concept of physical access is the concept that information retrieval is not site-dependent; it is potentially a multi-site enterprise that crosses nations and continents.

How do you use it?

Having answered the questions "What is it?" and "What does it say?", it is appropriate to ask a final question--"How do you use it?". Although each librarian will determine the most appropriate use of the *Model Statement*, a few guidelines might focus what must ultimately be an individually designed methodology. First, it is important to remember that the *Model Statement* targets no specific group of users--it can used with equal facility with new users, international students, or returning adult students. The *Model Statement* also focuses on the generalities of the information-gathering process rather than on traditional topic divisions, such as periodical indexes and reference sources. The key to the *Model Statement's* success lies in its flexibility--it can be used with equal ease when planning a computer-assisted instruction module or a series of 50-minute lectures.

The *Model Statement* will be most useful if one first engages in a bit of "front-end planning." "Front-end planning" usually consists of thinking of all those considerations that haunt designers at the end of a project--for example, designing a networked program for the Macintosh when your library decided to buy IBMs instead. It involves planning, as much as possible, for all the outside factors that can signal success or failure. Age group, prerequisite learning, and properly sequenced content are factors that should be determined before a program is designed. A "front-end plan" that will maximize the *Model Statement's* utility might include these steps:

1) Determine the purpose of the project--what behaviors should the user master as result of the instruction;
2) Identify potential user groups;
3) Determine the program areas of the *Model Statement* that are relevant for the purpose of the program, realizing that not all portions of the *Model Statement* will be equally important for each project;
4) Select appropriate terminal objectives for each area;
5) Develop locally-determined enabling objectives that whose achievement will indicate successful instruction.

When properly used with the appropriate set of expectations, the *Model Statement of Objectives* can be an important tool in the planning of an instructional program. The following papers illustrate how the *Model Statement* can be used to plan for two very different instructional situations.

Application of the Model Statement to a Basic Information Access Skills Program At Penn State University

Carol A. Wright
The Pennsylvania State University

The *Model Statement of Objectives* provides a cognitive structure for the development of instructional programs for many levels and subject disciplines. This chapter will focus on the application of the *Model Statement* to a Basic Information Access Skills program developed at Penn State, including:

- a definition of basic skills
- a review of the Penn State environment
- the process of instructional planning and design used
- a description of the prototype computer-assisted instruction module created
- comments on the relationship of a basic skills program to the total instructional program.

What Are Basic Information Access Skills?

The process of formulating a prescribed, identifiable body of basic concepts and skills has become a compelling and popular activity in many quarters of education. With so much information to teach, educators seek to define that content which forms the base of understanding of a field of study.

Librarians are faced with the conundrum of developing a core of 'basic' concepts which will create a firm base on which students can build future information-gathering activities. The combined effect of the expanding volume of information and expanding technological access to information has radically altered the scope and definition of what can be considered basic. The fundamental definition of basic should be flexible to accommodate an ever-expanding base of minimum-level competencies and new technologies.

Basic information skills are those which empower students to understand the broad organizational structure of the resources facilities and services at their disposal, which suggest the range of possibilities for information retrieval that exist, and which allow the student to ask intelligent questions during the information gathering process.

Recently, talk of 'basic skills' has prompted discussions of the definition of 'Information Literacy.' The notion of attempting to codify a body of knowledge into a literacy document--witness scientific literacy, math literacy, historical literacy--has generated heated debate, but a beneficial effect of the controversy has been attempts to define the concept of 'literacy.' Use of the term literacy has extended beyond the traditional meaning of being able to read and write, to a much broader, less easily defined meaning, explained by E.D. Hirsch in his introduction to the *Dictionary of Cultural Literacy*[1]. He defines literacy simply as the 'ability to communicate with strangers' that is, a common base on which we share and communicate and build knowledge. He describes the two essential characteristics of literacy as 'identification' and 'definition'. These two essential characteristics--identification and definition--are likewise fundamental elements of a basic information access skills program because they allow students to create mental maps, or frameworks for future learning, and are the base from which students may make important generalizations about the information search.

The need for effective instruction in basic information access skills has never been more urgent than at present. While some excellent examples of successful basic instruction are well known, basic instruction is more often structured around a series of artificial exercises where students manipulate pre-selected sources to complete narrow assignments, with questionable transfer of learning to other information retrieval situations. We can and must do better to design programs which create proficient library users.

The *Model Statement of Objectives* contributed to the development of Penn State's basic skills project by describing the broad concepts of information access. It is its value as a literacy document which establishes its connection to basic as well as more advanced instruction. Note that we call our project, not basic *library skills*, but rather basic *information access* skills. It was the *Model Statement* which in part suggested the base for this broadened concept.

The Penn State Environment

Penn State University consists of a main campus at University Park in the geographic center of the state, 18 two-year and associate institutions, one four-year college, one graduate center, and a medical school. Our total enrollment in 1989 was 70,031 students, with 37,600 at the main campus. Our student/librarian ratio across the PSU system is 653:1, a proportion which seriously limits our opportunities for extensive direct student contact, especially at the basic introductory level. Introductory library skills are presently taught through a self-paced workbook which is a required component of English 15 (and English 30, the honors equivalent). This is our basic freshman writing course, which averages 90 sections each semester at the main campus. An agreement with the English Department states that students must successfully complete the Workbook to pass the course. All students are required to take English 15/30 during their first or second semester, so that they complete the workbook early in their academic experience. No prior proficiencies are assumed; there is no mechanism for 'testing out' of the workbook, because one of the primary goals is the physical orientation to our facilities and the location of materials, best accomplished in a 'hands-on' environment.

English 15/30 seeks to develop effective expository and persuasive writing skills in a number of various rhetorical situations. The degree to which class assignments directly incorporate workbook experiences varies among instructors, but each student is eventually responsible for using the online catalog and for finding periodical and newspaper articles for class projects which require them to gather data and evidence in evaluative, persuasive, proposal, and descriptive writing assignments. Many classes may, for example, analyze the pathos, logos and ethos of Martin Luther King's "Letter From Birmingham City Jail," and may be required to find supporting newspaper and editorial articles from that period. Others may search for supporting data to argue the merits of issues such as higher minimum wage.

For some time it was apparent that the workbook relied upon a very mechanical manipulation of sources, focusing on how to USE sources, but lacking a broader conceptual base. Present workbook goals and objectives are very conditional and reflect the emphasis on mechanical manipulation. In addition to having students explore and become familiar with the library environment, typical goals are:

> "Given a periodical index, a student will identify an appropriate periodical article and locate that article in the library;"
> "Given a subject, a student will use the subject tracings and the shelf command to complete comprehensive search of the PSU online catalog."

These narrow goals are not unusual in a workbook environment where experiences and responses must be controlled.

Several factors were responsible for a re-examination of the substance and delivery of basic skills instruction:

1) The national debate on the quality of undergraduate instruction, general education and basic skills has received much attention at Penn State, and we wanted to participate in campus-wide efforts to improve instruction;

[handwritten note overlaid: "Things to do, ① Get booklet ② Ask for cover sheet."]

2) Penn State is moving toward an aggressive "Writing Across the Curriculum" initiative. Anticipating heavy library involvement, we wanted to upgrade efforts at the basic level.
3) The increased availability and popularity of electronic databases demanded basic level instruction.
4) The Penn State Center for Academic Computing provides grants for professional and technical support for faculty development of computer assisted instruction. The University Libraries felt that CAI technology would allow development of abstract and conceptual thought not possible in our present workbook. A grant was given from this computer support unit to assist with project development.

Instructional Planning and Design Process

The strategy to define the content of a basic skills curriculum was to first attempt to enumerate the total range of skills within the information access process and to plot levels of performance for each skill or concept. From this global list could be extracted skills identified as basic. In the literature review, we hoped to find a checklist or outline from which we could establish our list of skills. The *Model Statement* was just such a checklist.

The *Model Statement* is composed of four content areas:

1) how information is identified and defined by experts;
2) how information sources are structured;
3) how information sources are intellectually accessed by users;
4) how information sources are physically organized.

In the spirit of the *Model Statement,* which recommends flexibility, selection, and modification, these four were expanded into seven more narrowly defined content areas. These seven are:

I. Literature Formats
    (identifying literature characteristics and formats, including audience, purpose, scope etc., distinguishing the literature itself from its bibliographic access points.)

II. Literature Access Points
    (selecting and using print and non-print indexes, catalogs and reference and summary sources)

III. Physical Access
> (retrieving the information; determining specific locations and availability)

IV. Question Analysis
> (determining the components of a question)

V. Organization of Disciplines/Scholarly Communication Patterns
> (identifying the literature characteristics of a specific discipline)

VI. Information Evaluation
> (selecting and applying appropriate criteria to assess the value of a source)

VII. Physical Orientation
> (locating collections and services)

The link to the *Model Statement* is clear. We chose to reorder our content into these seven areas, and in this order, because to us they reflected a progression of conceptual development. "Physical Orientation" was intentionally placed last because we felt that students first needed to know the 'what and why' of information structure before knowing where things were located.

Next came the task of identifying what constituted the basic level within each section. We began to devise many lists, but they were all too linear and did not reflect levels of sophistication and performance within each concept. A grid which would list content vertically and describe proficiency levels horizontally was the next choice. We planned to place every concept at its' appropriate level, and then extract those applicable to the basic level. At the same time, our literature review revealed the work of Leon and Diane Nahl-Jakobovits[2] which studied the application of learning domains, first described by Bloom, Krathwohl and others[3] to library user behaviors. These first three learning domains are:

- cognitive domain [the intellectual learning level] which describes what one knows. This is the traditional focus of instruction.
- affective domain [emotional and attitudinal learning level] which describes what one feels. This domain, for example, accounts for 'library anxiety' described by Constance Mellon.[4]
- psychomotor domain. [physical learning level] which is important to consider as library facilities become more complex and as various technologies are required for access to information.

The Jakobovits make a compelling argument for the value of designing instruction to satisfy all three learning domains. They charted, in a nine-cell grid, user behaviors by learning domains and skill levels. From their work we realized the necessity of incorporating learning domain theory into our curriculum planning, and the result is the Information Access Skills Matrix. Further discussion about the Information Access Skills Matrix and its application to our basic skills program is described in the Summer 1990 issue of *Research Strategies*.[5] Figure 1 illustrates the structure of the matrix. Each of the seven content areas have similarly been plotted within the matrix configuration. Specific curricular content is then further elaborated and defined in the "Expanded Content Matrix." Figure 2, for example, illustrates content taught for electronic indexes.

From the matrix it emerges that the 'basic' orientation level is characterized by behaviors such as "Defining appropriate terminology;" "Recognizing characteristics of ...; "Recognize existence and function of ... ". Plotting skills within proficiency level and learning domain was particularly revealing because it showed that most skills typically taught in basic instruction programs were placed in the matrix's second column, at level two (Interaction--or, manipulation of sources.) It is rather the initial defining and characterizing process that broadens the conceptual base and is the essence of basic skills.

Of what direct value was the *Model Statement* in instructional design? First, it was particularly important for the inclusion of content number 5--"Organization of Disciplines and Scholarly Communication Patterns." This may seem to extend beyond the traditional definition of 'basic', but there is value, even at this early instructional stage, in identifying and defining the relationship of discipline organization to the information gathering process. As students study within each of the disciplines, they are taught and encouraged to concentrate on narrow areas of interest and they therefore fail to see the linkages in knowledge. This disjointed, unconnected learning is one of the criticisms of the college experience observed by Ernest Boyer in *College: The Undergraduate Experience in America*, a 1987 study published by the Carnegie Foundation for the Advancement of Teaching.[6] We have a wonderful opportunity to create an umbrella for these linkages with instruction in information literacy at this early stage. The identification and definition of the characteristics of disciplines is appropriate for basic level instruction. It creates a natural intellectual base on which to design instruction about access sources and establishes a framework upon which more advanced instruction can build. This introductory treatment of discipline analysis is also the springboard from which characteristics of information can be discussed. Students need this understanding of how information is generated, and will use it to make important distinctions in the information evaluation process.

The second reason the Model Statement was important was in focusing attention on literature formats. This helps highlight the parallel relationship of information with bibliographic access to that information. Analysis of the characteristics of literature formats is also the foundation for subsequent information evaluation activities.

Third, the *Model Statement* helped change our approach to teaching controlled vocabulary. It prompted us to include a comparison of 'free text' vs. controlled vocabulary, variations in terms used among sources, the value of maintaining a search log, and the use of subject headings in helping to define a topic.

Prototype CAI Module

The faculty support grant allowed the development of three CAI modules written in PC Pilot, a simple authoring language which supports color graphics. The program incorporates concepts outlined on the matrix, with the storyline premised on a team of three students who need to find materials for their assignment. The three developmental modules discuss Periodicals, the Online Catalog, and Reference and Summary Sources. Most screens are divided into three sections, with two windows at the top dedicated to graphics, sample text, summaries, etc. The bottom half of the screen is reserved for 'dialogue'--the conversation, discoveries and conclusions of the students. The program incorporates heavy use of interactivity, reminders and summary screens. Plans call for the program to be run on the Banyan network on the University's mainframe, so that students will have access from any computer lab on campus. An exam is incorporated in the program, with questions computer-selected at random. All responses are recorded on the mainframe so that we'll be able to trace patterns of student response, and monitor and respond to any programming difficulties. Final student results are to be sent to the instructor. Successful completion will be required, just as it is now for the workbook.

The Periodicals module, the first to be developed, was field-tested on two sections of English 15, before they had completed the workbook. Students reported strong positive feedback on content, presentation style, and computer delivery. The same students were queried informally at the very end of the semester after they had completed the workbook and had used the library for their assignments. They reported that they learned important concepts from the CAI module, but that they also strongly valued the hands-on experience that the workbook provided--physically walking through the building, handling materials, performing exercises, etc. The 'physical' component promoted confidence and made the learning concrete. The students supported the use of the CAI module content to expand the instructional base, but strongly advocated also keeping a 'hands-on' experience in the program. This reaction is predictable--it supports the importance of designing instruction which focuses on the affective domain where people need to feel comfortable and competent in their environment.

Relationship of Basic Skills to a Total Instructional Program

Students who are secure in the knowledge that they have broad concepts in place to help them identify, access, and manipulate information sources are most likely to use those sources when needed. The time to learn a new set of skills is not when those skills are needed to affect performance on another project. Students need to know early in their academic career how to learn about what is available. They need to know the existence of and be comfortable with the manipulation of information which can support their study and enhance their performance.

The implications for instructional planning are clear--if we can be sure that basic skills are in place, then more appropriate advance teaching can be planned. For us at Penn State, this means being active in the 'Writing Across the Curriculum' program, and in other targeted disciplines.

Basic skills appear simple. The danger in research, particularly in an online environment, is that students will retrieve *something*. Firm grounding in basic skills will help them evaluate the information they've retrieved.

In a January 1990 forecast for the decade, Brown University's Vartan Gregorian said:

> '... one of the scourges of the 1990's will be mental grid-
> lock in the form of undigested information ...'[7]

Through Basic Skills, we have an opportunity to help students make sense of the information they encounter.

NOTES

1. E.D. Hirsch, Joseph F. Kett, and James Trefil. *The Dictionary of Cultural Literacy* (Boston, MA: Houghton Mifflin, 1988).

2. Leon Jakobovits and Diane Nahl-Jakobovits, "Learning the Library: Taxonomy of Skills and Errors," *College and Research Libraries* 48 (May 1987): 203-214.

3. Benjamin S. Bloom, ed., *Taxonomy of Educational Objectives: the Classification of Educational Goals. Handbook I: Cognitive Domain* (New York: David McKay, 1956); David R. Krathwohl, Benjamin S. Bloom, and Bertram B. Masia, *Taxonomy of Educational Objectives: The Classification of Educational Goals. Handbook II: Affective Domain* (New York: David McKay, 1964).

4. Constance Mellon, "Library Anxiety: a Grounded Theory and Its Development," *College and Research Libraries* 47 (March 1986): 160-165.

5. Carol Wright and Mary Ellen Larson, "Basic Information Access Skills: Curriculum Design using a Matrix Approach," *Research Strategies* 8 (Summer 1990): 104-115.

6. Ernest L. Boyer, *College: the Undergraduate Experience In America* (New York: Harper Row, 1987).

7. Vartan Gregorian quoted in "Periscope: Education," *Newsweek* 115 (January 8, 1990): 6.

FIGURE 1
INFORMATION ACCESS SKILLS MATRIX

II. Literature Access Points	Level I-Orientation	Level II-Interaction
A. LIAS (Online Catalog) Affective	**A1** • Willing to learn use of an online catalog	**A2** • Demonstrate confidence in using an online system • Willing to seek LIAS data as necessary
Cognitive	**C1** • Define LIAS • Distinguish from other online systems • Identify scope of LIAS database • Identify LIAS commands • Recognize existence and purpose of a unique vocabulary that controls subject access • Identify information elements on LIAS screen	**C2** • Select LIAS use appropriately • Use LIAS commands correctly • Use appropriate headings for subject access • Use appropriate subdivisions of main subject heading • Use LCSH to assist in topic definition to expand/narrow topic
Sensorimotor	**S1** • Locate LIAS function keys on keyboard	**S2** • Use LIAS function keys appropriately

Figure 1 (cont.)

II. Literature Access Points	Level I-Orientation	Level II-Interaction
B. Periodical Indexes - Print Affective	**A1** ● Willing to learn use of indexes/abstracts as literature access points	**A2** ● Demonstrate confidence in use of indexes/abstracts ● Is willing to use as necessary
Cognitive	**C1** ● Define appropriate terminology ● Recognize purpose of bibliographic control for periodical information ● Recognize characteristics of general/specialized index ● Recognize existence and purpose of unique vocabulary that controls subject ● Identify common elements within a citation	**C2** ● Choose appropriate index/abstract for topic ● Use correct vocabulary to locate appropriate citation ● Compile list of appropriate vocabulary to narrow/expand search
Sensorimotor	**S1** ● Identify information elements within citations ● Identify relationship between citation and article	**S2** ● Find article from citation information

FIGURE 2
INFORMATION ACCESS SKILLS MATRIX
[EXPANDED CONTENT]

II.   Literature Access Points

C. Electronic Indexes

C-1

● Define appropriate terminology
--index
--electronic
--online
--compact disc/CD-ROM
--free text
--Boolean logic
--search commands

....

C-1

● Recognize characteristics of electronic databases (CD-ROM)
--data is stored on disc
--accessed through terminal
--computer can be searched by any word in the database
--search terms can be combined
--Usually gives a citation, not the article text
--does not allow scanning in the same way a print source does

C-2

●   Selection based on scope and purpose

....

C-1

● Recognize differences in system software
--CD-ROM indexes are searched by many different companies
--system commands vary; several CD-ROMs (and command systems) may be used in one search

C-2

●   Use system commands as appropriate
●   Follow instructions at each terminal

....

C-1

● Recognize existence and use of free text and controlled vocabulary
--searching free text can enhance access to information
--searching subject headings only can help narrow a broad topic

C-2

●   Use controlled and free text vocabulary appropriately
--varying search results are obtained from each strategy
--each search requires different search techniques

....

C-1

● Recognize function of Boolean operators.
● Search terms can be combined to manipulate (broaden or narrow) a search

C-2

●   Use Boolean operators to create search statements
"or" - expands search results
"and" - narrows search results
"not" - narrows search results

....

C-1

● Recognize structure of electronic database records
--each citation is composed of several data elements

C-2

●   Prepare search based on knowledge of electronic database record structure
●   Searches can be refined by limiting to selected portions of the record

Understanding The Present In The Past: Instruction In The Use Of Original Source Materials

Rutherford W. Witthus
University of Colorado at Denver

A Side Trip to Colorado

In the summer of 1858, a man from Georgia named William Green Russell discovered a small amount of gold near the mouth of Dry Creek at the foot of the Rocky Mountains in what is now Colorado. The placer strike was cleaned out in a short time and Russell's party moved on. The news of the discovery, however, spread east to Kansas City, where the headlines proclaimed the New Eldorado. Thousands of gold seekers planned to leave for the gold fields the following Spring of 1859. An enterprising group of people from Kansas had already established Montana City at the site of the Russell strike but, finding little gold and before the first cabin could be built, its citizens moved further down the river, where they laid out the townsite of St. Charles in the fall of 1858. Fearing the impending harsh winter, members of the St. Charles Town Company left their town site on the east side of Cherry Creek and headed back to Kansas, with plans to return the following spring.

At the same time, the Russell party (the ones who found the gold that started the rush) were driven from the mountains by the early snow. As they descended from the mountains, they saw the wagons of the St. Charles party leaving for Kansas and decided that they could cash in on the gold seekers who would return in the Spring. On the west side of Cherry Creek, they established a town called Auraria, named after their hometown in Georgia. Auraria means "a place of gold." Within a few years, the town of Auraria was incorporated into the east bank settlement, which by then was known as Denver City.

Over the years, the name Auraria disappeared, but the area, known in Denver as the Near West Side, was home to a diverse population of German-, English-, Italian-, and Spanish-speaking people. Each ethnic group established its own community, built its own church, and lived in relative harmony for nearly a century. As the residents became financially able to purchase newer houses, they moved away from the neighborhood, leaving many of their traditions and older relatives behind. In the 1960s, after nearly a century of activity, the neighborhood was in need of renewal. About the same time, the Colorado legislature decided to fund the establishment of an urban campus to house the

University of Colorado at Denver, Metropolitan State College of Denver (MSCD), and the Community College of Denver. The place chosen was the old town site of Auraria. Urban development meant urban displacement for many of the families of the Near West Side. The campus was finally constructed on the east bank of Cherry Creek across from downtown Denver and was named the Auraria Higher Education Center.

Bibliographic Instruction at Auraria

The diversity of population in the Auraria neighborhood was replaced with a diversity of students. Because the campus was home to community college students, undergraduates, master's, and doctoral candidates, cooperative programs such as bibliographic instruction needed to encompass diverse populations. In 1986, a bibliographic instruction program was established with the Metropolitan State College of Denver English Department. The program reached all MSCD students by integrating two one-hour sessions of library instruction into 72 sections of English 102 each semester. This large and almost too successful program was developed and coordinated by Lori Arp, chair of the committee which revised the *Model Statement of Objectives for Academic Bibliographic Instruction* adopted in 1989 by ACRL.

In any large-scale instruction program, there are sure to be variations on the central theme. One of the variations is taught by Dr. Sandra Doe, whose English 102 sequence is entitled *Writing as a Way of Knowing*. During the semester, her students use the Auraria campus as their laboratory for generating ideas. As part of the course, students are asked to use original source materials relating to the history of Auraria. Confronted with this assignment and similar ones from history professors, the Head of Archives and Special Collections and the Coordinator of Bibliographic Instruction decided it was time to investigate how one might approach the problem of instruction in the use of original source materials.

Archives and Manuscripts

Archives and manuscripts have traditionally been separated from other materials in libraries -- and for good reasons. They contain different kinds of information, they are created differently, they look and act differently, and they are organized differently. One characteristic they have in common with other library materials is that they contain information. And not only do they contain information, they contain a very special kind of information -- first-hand accounts of contemporary events, records of individual lives, daily details of business transactions, and papers documenting the generation of organizational and governmental policy. Manuscripts generally refer to the papers of an individual or a family. Manuscripts may include diaries, letters, photographs, speeches, and legal papers. When you write a letter or an entry in a diary, you are describing what is happening or has just happened or is about to happen. When you shoot a photograph, you are graphically recording a moment. Letters and diaries are a rich source of contemporary information about an individual or a family.

Archives, on the other hand, are "the preserved documentary records of a corporate body [or] a governmental agency ... that are the direct result of administrative or organizational activity of the originating body and that are maintained according to their original provenance."[1] The key word, and the term that requires some explanation, is *provenance*.

"Provenance is the principle that holds that archival material should be arranged according to its organic source rather than by its subject or other category."[2] Compare this to what we usually do in libraries. We anaylze the subject of a book, periodical, film, map, or any other library item in order to classify it. We classify it so it can be shelved near other materials on the same subject. By doing this, we allow users to browse physically by subject in a *single* area of the library. We also analyze the subjects of library materials in order to create bibliographic records in a catalog. We want the user to be able to call up all catalog records of items on the same subject. By doing this, we allow users to browse intellectually the *entire* library by subject.

In an archives, we neither describe nor arrange materials by subject. Description generally focusses on the activities and functions of the creator of a group of records and the types of documents created. While new cataloging rules allow multiple subject headings to be added to an archival catalog record, the main descriptive activity still revolves around the function and structure of the records.[3] While not specifically opposed to content description of documents, archivists usually maintain that the volume of material does not allow one to spend time analyzing the subjects of all the documents in their custody.

The principle of provenance dictates that we attempt to maintain or recreate the arrangement of records as they were in the office of origin. We do this for a good reason: "archival documents generally make sense only as part of a group of records. Record groups reflect the many activities which created them and may be useful for many subjects."[4] The groups of related documents also create the context in which the subject of individual documents can be understood. Record groups are further divided into series (minutes, directives, regulations, ledgers, etc.), which describe specific activities or functions of the office of origin.

Because archival records are created at the time of an activity, archives are another rich source of contemporary information about an organization or a government.

Use of Archives and Manuscripts

When a user comes to the archives seeking information on the buildings which originally stood on the site of the present campus, the archivist attempts to transform this subject query into functional terms relating to organizational activity. In other words, the archivist uses a process of inference to determine which organizational unit is most likely to have jurisdiction over an activity that might have generated information on that particular topic.[5] If the buildings were constructed during the first years of settlement, no building permits exist because none were required. However, the constitution of the Auraria Town Company specifies that all construction in Auraria needed Board approval. The records of the Auraria Town Company, which operated under that constitution, contain petitions by various shareholders and property owners requesting approval of various types of structures on certain lots. Hotels, houses, ice houses, and other improvements are mentioned, along with owner's names and building locations.

These records are held together by the fact that they were created in the course of business of the Auraria Town Company. The hundreds of names, the hundreds of locations, the types of buildings are named in the catalog description of the collection as a whole. Yet we are able to locate this information by knowing that certain types of records contain specific kinds of information; for example, town company minutes contain names of inhabitants and types of buildings. By knowing the function of the company through its constitution, the researcher is able to locate information by knowing what might be included in various types of documents. The principle of provenance requires the archivist to maintain the Auraria Town Company minutes in the order in which they were created, not to rearrange them according to shareholder, petitioner, or any other category.

The traditional reference interview in archives required the user to bring sufficient subject expertise to the archivist, who then, with the help of finding aids, tried to remember which collections might contain relevant information. Today, however, with the ever-increasing use of automation in the archives, users arrive in the archives with collection-level records from the online public access catalogs. The records do not look like bibliographic records -- some contain organizational histories, biographies, and a multitude of subject and form headings. Either automated systems must include an expert component to translate user subject queries into organizational activity statements, or the users must be instructed in the use of original source materials in order to retrieve relevant papers and records. Because these expert systems are not yet in place, users of original source materials must be taught to think inferentially.

Why don't archivists give in and organize their materials by subject so that users can retrieve information from archives and libraries in similar ways? The great archives theorist, T. R. Schellenberg, advises the archivist to "resist any efforts on the part of scholars to induce him to arrange records according to any abstract system of universal subject classification."[6] Because users want information generated by the activity that created the records, "retaining records in the order generated by the original activity allows access through analysis of function, a powerful mode of access."[7]

Instruction in the Use of Original Source Materials

Some of the objectives of bibliographic instruction are to present the user of information with the structure, physical organization, and intellectual access to information. With that background, the user develops various processes to gather information. Successful bibliographic instruction expects users to learn the basic principles of classification and cataloging, to use subject entries from catalogs, and to retrieve books from the shelves. Can users be expected to understand the difference between libraries and archives, to use the principle of provenance to facilitate retrieval, to infer subjects from functions, and to request the appropriate documents from the archives? The use of original source materials in a freshman writing course provided a vehicle not only to answer these questions, but also to use the *Model Statement* to articulate instructional objectives for the provision of specific skills.

The first major activity in the sequence *Writing as a Way of Knowing*[8] requests students to experience the campus first-hand by walking around and recording their impressions. Then, they are asked to choose one historic building on campus to use as a focus. At this point, the library and its resources are presented to the students. Revising somewhat the three-part research strategy introduced by Betsy Wilson and Lori Arp[9] in 1984, the students are presented with a search strategy based on a series of three questions: What is your topic? What kind of information do you need? And what is the time-frame of the information needed? The distinction between retrospective and contemporary information is introduced and becomes particularly meaningful when the student attempts to locate contemporary information in 19th and early 20th century newspapers relating to their chosen building or person. The concept that the past also had a present is often new to freshmen students. The distinction between retrospective and contemporary information sources helps them understand that concept.

The next activity involves the use of references. A bibliography of books and articles relating to the history and architecture of Denver is distributed to the class. Students are asked to find out as much as they can about the *recorded* history of their building and its inhabitants by using secondary sources.

Up to this point, we respond to many of the objectives of bibliographic instruction -- how information is identified and defined, how library information sources are structured and intellectually accessed, how books and periodicals are physically organized -- and we attempt to relay this information at the time of need.

One of the objectives of this class is to encourage students to use original source materials. As we discovered earlier, use of archives and manuscripts requires an inferential process to transform a subject query into functional terms. We have devised a non-library exercise to help the students learn inferential thinking. Students read a chapter from *Artifacts and the American Past* by Thomas J. Schlereth entitled "Above-Ground Archaeology: Discovering a Community's History through Local Artifacts."[10] After reading Schlereth, they again look at the campus, and make a list of topics, with questions they *might* ask to find further information on the topics. These questions are their first attempt to infer functions from subjects. Some examples from a student studying the historic churches on campus might make the process easier to follow: What kind of stone was used to construct St. Elizabeth's? Is the stone native to this area? Why does St. Cajetan's look different from St. Elizabeth's, even though both are Roman Catholic churches? Who were the people attending these churches and how did their cultures differ? What did the area look like before the churches were built? The student was asked to determine which disciplines would most likely produce *published* information that would answer his questions. His initial questions led him into the disciplinary literature of geology, sociology, religion, and anthropology.

After completing an initial search of library materials, students receive instruction in what constitutes archival material, how it is structured, organized, and accessed. Particular emphasis is placed on the various forms of archival material and the functions associated with each: why do individuals write diaries; why do companies keep ledgers; what is the difference between a memorandum and a policy statement; why do people correspond with each other? Diaries are intended to record the personal reminiscences of an individual for that individual's own use. Letters are intended to convey an individual's thoughts and feelings to another person. Account books are intended to record and report statistical information about the finances of an individual or organization. And, likewise, all types of materials found in an archives are intended to convey particular kinds of information.

Next, students are asked to look again at their questions and determine what kind of contemporary documentary source might answer some of their questions. For questions about the churches, we discuss building permits, supplier's catalogs, church records, early photographs, and newspaper accounts. The next, and usually the most difficult, assignment requests the students to determine where they might find documents and other sources that might answer their questions. We help the students find repository guides and online citations for other collections in the Denver metropolitan area. We hope that archivists and special collections librarians in the other Denver repositories are now asked meaningful questions. Rather than a simple subject query: Do you have anything on St. Elizabeth's Church? we hope they are able to combine form of material with functional analysis, and ask: Do any of your collections contain building supplier's catalogs from the 1890s? Or, does the library have building permits from 1890? Or, does the photographic collection contain any photographs of West Denver or Auraria from the 19th century?

Rewriting the Terminal Objectives of the Model Statement

The student must understand the kinds of material found in an archives and the principle of provenance in order to engage in meaningful archival research. That is one of the objectives for this sequence of classes. Let us, then, use the *Model Statement* to state these objectives. We start by rewriting already familiar terminal objectives found in the *Model Statement*.

> T1. The user understands how the organizational content of recorded information sources is structured and how this knowledge can help determine the usefulness of the source.
>> a. The user understands the importance of evaluating the author's credentials.

When rewritten, this subpoint addresses the principle of provenance:

> *a. The user understands the importance of knowing who created, gathered, or changed the records and for what purpose.*

Likewise, the archives principle of respect for original order may be taught by using another subpoint under T1.

>> f. The user recognizes the organization or arrangement of an information source may affect its value.

When rewritten, this subpoint reads:

> *f. The user recognizes that the original order of a collection may relay important information about the creator.*

The student must also understand the various forms of material found in an archives and the kind of information each form communicates. Under General Objective 1, How information is identified and defined by experts,

> T3. The user recognizes that disciplines use specific methods to communicate information.

becomes

> *T3. The user recognizes that individuals and organizations use specific methods to communicate information.*

The enabling objectives associated with this terminal objective include discussions of the various types of documentary information and the individual or organizational functions they reflect.

Retrieval of archival materials depends on access points like any other type of information. We include in the subpoints under the terminal objective describing access points:

> *The user recognizes that form of material and function for which it was created are commonly used access points for archival materials.*

Where libraries use content-related access points (names, subjects, geographic place names, chronology), archives use provenance-related access points (form of material and function). In a similar manner, relevant parts of the *Model Statement* are rewritten or amended to include elements necessary to understand the use of original source materials.

One instruction session in the sequence is held in the Archives and Special Collections room of the library. We review the search strategy presented in the earlier session. We then expand the concept of contemporary information to include archival and manuscript material. A show-and-tell of material relating to the student's research allows them to view and use examples of various forms of contemporary documentary materials: diaries, letters, ledgers, legal documents, and photographs.

The research papers produced in this course are juried by a peer group in the class and, if accepted for publication, are housed in the archives. The papers may then be used by future classes, thereby creating a community of Auraria scholars. This also serves the mission of the archives, which is to document various activities on campus, including student scholarly activity.

Archives-Library Interaction

The advantage of using the *Model Statement* for planning instruction in the use of original source materials is that it allows the instructor to relate provenance-based retrieval to the more familiar subject-based retrieval by using identical general objectives and similar terminal objectives. In this program, we expand the idea of contemporary information to include archives and manuscripts as contemporary documentary information. We introduce the principle of provenance and display the kinds of material generally found in an archives. We present and practice inferential thinking as it relates to archival research. We encourage the use of original source materials in conjunction with primary and secondary materials in research papers. At the same time, we do not expect freshman writing students to prepare theses and dissertations. Mark Greene, former college archivist at Carleton College, notes that "the bulk of undergraduate use of the [college] archives is not in the form of extensive research...From photographs being used as teaching aids to yearbooks being examined for examples of the psychology of prejudice, brief 'raids' into archival sources constitute legitimate use."[11]

Throughout the sequence, students use the resources of both the library and the archives, with some understanding of their differences and similarities. William J. Maher of the University of Illinois at Urbana/Champaign Archives suggests that librarians and archivists should view themselves and their resources "as their users see them -- merely as different facets of the totality of information resources."[12] Maher stresses the important lessons students learn when they move between published and unpublished sources: "...how knowledge is developed, how it is distilled into books, and how it might be questioned, dissected, and reassessed in light of additional evidence. The laboratories for this important educational process are the campus libraries and archives..."[13]

If the success of a program can be measured in student enthusiasm, this program is successful. Students enter the class with the usual low to non-existent level of expectation and enthusiasm accorded English 102 classes. When they discover they will spend time researching the history of the campus, they become further dismayed and threaten withdrawal. By the end of the semester, however, many students confess that this English class has been special. This is how one student put it: "I expected to write a few research papers on current world problems or study the writings of some special somebody that I had never heard of. Instead, the experience of studying my immediate surroundings led me to a subject that I never thought I would be interested in -- the Tivoli-Union Brewing Company. At first, searching for information related to my subject was slow and tedious. After the first few assignments, my searching became even slower and more tedious. I uncovered information that few other persons knew about. It was there to be found by anyone but *I* found it! Discovering very small bits of data here and there, I managed to piece together a lifetime already lived by others. Much of what we know as human beings is learned in the same way. Over time, we pick up little bits of information, then somewhere along the line, we link it with other bits of information and interpret it to suit our lives."

Overall, we are pleased with most of the research papers and fascinated by many. Both students and faculty on an urban campus tend to overdose on current social issues. The introduction of contemporary documentary information into a mainstream bibliographic instruction program creates an interesting focus and, at the same time, expands the horizons of the student. After the second week, not one student wanted to write a paper on abortion, AIDS, or the homeless. That fact alone brings joy to an archivist's and librarian's soul.

Notes

1. Steven L. Hensen, comp. *Archives, Personal Papers, and Manuscripts: A Cataloging Manual for Archival Repositories, Historical Societies, and Manuscript Libraries*. 2nd edition. Chicago: Society of American Archivists, 1989, p. 9.

2. Gerald F. Brown, Wilmer O. Maedke, and Mary F. Robek, *Information and Records Management*. London: Glencoe Press, 1974, p. 438.

3. For an excellent comparison of the approaches taken by libraries and archives to analysis of, description of, and access to information, see Mary Jo Pugh, "The Illusion of Omniscience: Subject Access and the Reference Archivist," *American Archivist* 45 (Winter 1982): 33-44.

4. Pugh, p. 33.

5. The author strongly recommends the work of Richard H. Lytle and David Bearman, whose discussions of retrieval in archival systems has influenced much of this paper. Richard H. Lytle, "Intellectual Access to Archives: I. Provenance and Content Indexing Methods of Subject Retrieval," *American Archivist* 43 (Winter 1980): 64-75; Richard H. Lytle, "Intellectual Access to Archives: II. Report of an Experiment Comparing Provenance and Content Indexing Methods of Subject Retrieval," *American Archivist* 43 (Spring 1980): 191-206; David A. Bearman and Richard H. Lytle, "The Power of the Principle of Provenance," *Archivaria* 21 (Winter 1985-86): 14-27.

6. T.R. Schellenberg, *Modern Archives: Principles and Techniques*. Chicago: University of Chicago Press, 1956, p. 188.

7. Pugh, p. 34.

8. For further information on the syllabus for *Writing as a Way of Knowing*, contact Dr. Sandra Doe, English Department, Campus Box 32, Metropolitan State College of Denver, 1006 11th Street, Denver, CO 80204.

9. Lori L. Arp and Lizabeth A. Wilson, "Library Instructor's View--Theoretical," *Research Strategies* 2 (Winter 1984): 16-22. Because archives and manuscript collections are, more often than not, multidisciplinary, the Arp/Wilson question *What subject discipline is involved?* was changed to *What is your topic?* to allow students to connect with the activities and functions of the creators of the documents.

10. Thomas J. Schlereth, *Artifacts and the American Past*. Nashville, Tenn.: American Association for State and Local History, [1980].

11. Mark A. Greene, "Using College and University Archives as Instructional Materials: A Case Study and an Exhortation," *Midwestern Archivist* 14, no. 1 (1989): 35.

12. William J. Maher, "Improving Archives-Library Relations: User-Centered Solutions to a Sibling Rivalry," *Journal of Academic Librarianship* 15 (January 1990): 358.

13. Maher, p. 358.

Poster Session Abstracts

The abstracts on the following pages are examples of how librarians have practically applied the *Model Statement* to library instruction programs at their institution.

Adapting the BI Model Statement of Objectives to be Used by the University of Maryland and College Park Libraries

Rebecca Jackson
Carleton Jackson
University of Maryland
College Park Libraries
College Park, Maryland

The University of Maryland and College Park Libraries created a committee composed of eight people from public service sites to adapt the *Model Statement* of Objectives. The committee divided library users into four groups and objectives were created for each group. Behavioral objectives were not used in the comprehensive statement, because it was felt that the constant changes in our libraries necessitated an objective statement that was flexible. In addition to creating objectives for user groups, we also created behavioral objectives for specific BI projects and programs. The accompanying outline is the result of the process to design standards for graduate students.

LIBRARY INSTRUCTION STANDARDS

GRADUATE STUDENTS

Introduction

Graduate students are expected to have mastered the essential general competencies for library use as stated in the Standards for Undergraduate Students, including use of services and facilities particular to UMCP Libraries. They develop in-depth information skills using advanced bibliographic tools in conjunction with analysis and synthesis of the information gathered.

Graduate students may encounter or undertake diverse methodologies relating to their disciplines. These methodologies will require different means to access and gather information, and students should be familiar with the various library research strategies/tools for the methodologies encountered in their fields of study.

I. How Information is identified and defined by experts.

General objective: The user understands how information is defined by experts, and recognizes how that knowledge can help determine the direction of his/her search for specific information.

A. The user recognizes that disciplines use different methodologies to access, analyze and communicate information.

B. The user recognizes that scholarly information sources go through various review processes to be accepted by the research community.

II. How information sources are structured and evaluated for their usefulness.

General objective: The user understands the importance of the organizational content, bibliographic structure, function, and use of information sources.

A. The user understands the importance of internal and external evidence in evaluating the usefulness of a work.

1. The user understands the importance of evaluating the author's credentials and incorporates this criterion in the synthesis of research material.

2. The user recognizes that the publisher's reputation may affect the usefulness of the source. The user recognizes that in periodical publications, the editorial review process influences the published information.

B. The user understands that unrecorded information sources, i.e., oral communication, exist. S/he recognizes the importance of the source's credentials and is able to evaluate this information to determine the source's credibility in relation to the topic.

C. The user understands how information sources are bibliographically organized and how this knowledge can help determine the usefulness of the source.

1.   The user understands that some sources may indirectly refer to other sources through the use of incomplete citations (implicit vs. explicit footnotes).

2.   The user understands the information provided within a citation and is able to evaluate the usefulness of the source by the citation.

III.   How information sources are intellectually accessed by users.

General objectives: The user can identify useful information from information sources or information systems.

A.   The user understands that certain elements of information called access points are accepted by the research community as the most pertinent through which to identify new information.

B.   The user recognizes that the use of access points other than author, title, or subject depends on the structure and format of the source used to identify new information.

1.   The user recognizes that additional access may be available through codes, categories, or mappings which may not be found in the cited document.

2.   The user recognizes that methodological and critical perspectives may be access points in some information sources (e.g., the Modern Language Association International Bibliography) and not in others. These may vary also between the print source and the online version.

C.   The user understands that there are a variety of information sources called access tools whose primary purpose is to identify other information sources through the use of access points.

IV.   How information sources are physically organized and accessed.

General objectives: The user understands the way collections of information sources are physically organized and accessed.

A.   The user understands that the campus library is not the only location through which to identify and retrieve necessary material.

1.   The user is able to obtain an item through Interlibrary Loan (document delivery) services.

2.   The user is aware that some sources cannot be loaned or reproduced, necessitating travel to use the source.

3.   The user can locate original materials (manuscripts, archives) pertinent to his/her field of research and is aware of protocol involved in using the facilities.

4.   The user understands that computerized information is available through remote access at other locations both on and off campus.

B.   The user understands that graduate students may have some special access privileges to some services and materials.

Bibliographic Instruction for Upper Level Transfer Students: An Approach Based on the Model Statement of Objectives for Bibliographic Instruction

Michael Miranda
State University of New York, Plattsburgh

The State University of New York (SUNY) College at Plattsburgh requires, as a component of its General Education Program, a one credit course entitled "Introduction to Library Research". The General Education program mandates that the course be taken within the first two semesters of residence at SUNY-Plattsburgh. As a result of changing demographics, an increasing percentage of students enrolled at SUNY-Plattsburgh are transfers from primarily two-year institutions. These junior and senior level transfer students were ill-served by a course conceived and designed for freshmen.

Clearly a change in the Bibliographic Instruction program was warranted but the form the new version of the course was to take required considerable study. A number of factors indicated that a discipline oriented, concept based, upper level version of the course would best meet our students' needs:

1) transfer students generally possess at least some minimal skills through their exposure to libraries at their first institution;

2) when transfer students arrive at SUNY-Plattsburgh they have selected a major and will be concentrating their efforts on completing their major requirements;

3) the comparative intellectual maturity of transfer students allows more latitude in the introduction of concepts.

This last factor convinced the designer of the course that the *Model Statement of Objectives for Bibliographic Instruction* would provide a suitable framework for the introduction and development of a concept based version of the course.

The result of this effort has been a more relevant course for the students and a higher level of satisfaction among the students. This first revised version, which was designed for Business/Economics students, has provided the model for the development of other discipline oriented versions of the course.

UNIT ONE

COMPONENTS OF THE INFORMATION WORLD

PRIMARY:

    Original research, letters, diaries, newspapers, financials, annual reports, etc.

SECONDARY:

    Uses primary sources, reports you write

TYPES OF INFORMATION

FACT:

    Generally accepted to be true

INTRODUCTORY/OBJECTIVE:

    Collection of Facts
    Both sides of controversies

SUBJECTIVE:

    Selective use of facts;
    matter of emphasis

DIVISIONS ARE NOT RIGID; THERE IS MUCH OVERLAP

DIFFERENT FORMATS - DIFFERENT FUNCTIONS:

    Monographs
    Periodicals
    Electronic

WHAT DO YOU NEED?

    Teacher's requirements
    Analyze the need

> This Unit introduces the students to the underlying concepts in the structure of information. The unit most closely relates to General Objectives 1 and 2 of the Model Statement.

UNIT TWO

TOPIC FORMATION/TOPIC ANALYSIS

WHAT MAKES FOR A GOOD RESEARCH TOPIC?
Substance
Controversy
Maturity

Instructor's guidelines, first and foremost, will shape your topic!

SIX DEADLY SINS:
Too Broad
Too Narrow
Too Technical
Single Source
Subjective
Cliche'

> Unit Two seeks to introduce the students to some of the considerations they will be faced with when determining the topics they will research. It includes a discussion of some of the most common problems and some helpful questions the student can ask themselves. It relates most closely to Terminal Objectives 4 and 5 under General Objective One.

All of the above are relative:
what's fine for one class may not be for another

TOPIC ANALYSIS:

What is your topic about?

Where is the information you need likely to be found?

Who are the major players in the development of your topic?

When are the important pieces of information on your topic likely to have been published?

The answers to these questions will change as your research evolves.

UNIT THREE

CORPORATE STRUCTURE/INFORMATION STRUCTURE

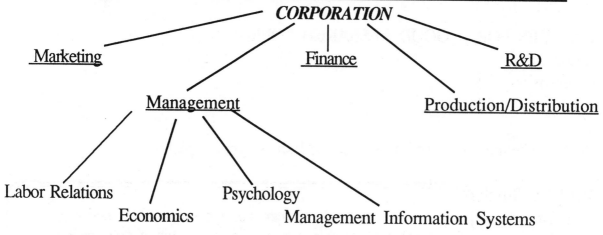

CORPORATION

Marketing   Finance   R&D

Management   Production/Distribution

Labor Relations   Economics   Psychology   Management Information Systems

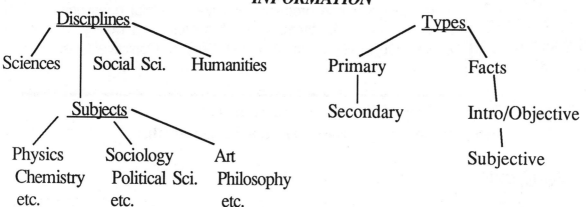

INFORMATION

Disciplines   Types

Sciences   Social Sci.   Humanities   Primary   Facts

Subjects   Secondary   Intro/Objective

Physics   Sociology   Art   Subjective
Chemistry   Political Sci.   Philosophy
etc.   etc.   etc.

Topics can be interdisciplinary;
Expand your horizons

INFORMATION ORGANIZATION:

Disciplines
Subjects
Classification

> The primary purpose of Unit Three is to get the students to look outside of their own field for some of the answers they will need. By demonstrating that a corporation consists of a variety of discplines we encourage the students to consider other areas of study as they might relate to the problem at hand. General Objective One is again the focus.

Systems of organization make libraries useful.

UNIT FOUR

GAINING ACCESS

Basic Access Points:
    Author - Editor, corporate, none
    Title - Full title, partial, key word
    Subject - Controlled vocabulary, key word
    Text - Word

Indexing Provides Access:
    Indexing rules
    Subject indexing - authority, controlled vocabulary vs. key word

Access source provides the first point analysis:
    Author - affiliation
    Length
    Date
    Bibliography/Index
    Can suggest other access points

COMPUTERIZED ACCESS CAN CHANGE EVERYTHING

> With this unit we arrive at what the students consider the "meat" of the course. We have laid the foundation for the student"s to actually start putting into action some of the conceptual ideas we have introduced. This unit begins the hands on portion of the course which the students find to be the most practical. General Objective Three is clearly the foundation for this unit. Additionally, the students gain more in depth exposure to the physical workings of the library itself which relates to General Objective Four.

UNIT FIVE

ELECTRONIC ACCESS

Boolean Searching

Free text:
What it is
Advantages: Any word, no rules to learn
Disadvantages: No control, indiscriminate

Controlled vocabulary:
What it is
Advantages: Ordered, relatively consistent, analytical
Disadvantages: Prescriptive, slow

Use of Thesaurii:

Symbolic Systems of Access:
SIC, Tax Code, Legal References

What do you use?
Evaluation of access options

This unit is actually a continuation of Unit Four. In addition to introducing the basics of Boolean searching and the comparison of free text to controlled vocabulary searching the symbolic systems of access that business students need to be familiar with are also introduced.. Unfortunately, at this time, a lot of the material is promissory as we have few electronic systems of use to the business students as yet. This Unit again relates primarily to General Objective Three.

UNIT SIX

CITATION AND ATTRIBUTION

Plagiarism

Style manuals

Review of course

The final unit is largely devoted to a review of all components of the course. We discuss the various style manuals and the serious implications of plagiarism. A significant portion of class time is devoted to discussing the Final Project which requires the students to simulate the workings of a corporate research department. This practical application of the principles learned plays a significant role in helping the students understand the.course and its objectives. Generally the students have been very satisfied with the course and find it valuable.

Using the BI Model Statement of Objectives to Integrate Concept-Based Bibliographic Instruction into the University of Detroit Core Curriculum

Shirley Black
University of Detroit Main Library
Detroit, Michigan

The *Model Statement* was used to compose goal and objectives statements specific to the needs of the students at the University of Detroit. The Bibliographic Instruction Committee composed general, terminal and enabling objectives to address five areas of concern:

- creation and organization of knowledge,

- critical thinking skills, intellectual access,

- librarian as resource,

- physical location.

An instructional design model describes the program components: needs assessment to identify student information needs at the University of Detroit, goal and objectives statements to serve as rationale for inclusion of information skills in the university core curriculum, and the design of concept-based instructional materials.

Goal and Objectives Statement for Bibliographic Instruction
University of Detroit Main Library

Goal Statement

A student, upon completion of a program of study, will make efficient and effective use of the available library material and staff in the identification and retrieval of material.

Area of Concern: Creation and Organization of Knowledge

General Objective: The student understands how ideas become part of recorded knowledge and how libraries organize that knowledge.

Terminal Objective 1. The student knows that there is a progression from lesser to greater formality in the recording of knowledge.

> **Enabling Objective:** The student traces the earliest published record of a given idea.

Terminal Objective 2. The student comprehends that libraries are organized according to the formats in which knowledge is recorded and that libraries have finding tools appropriate to each format.

> **Enabling Objective:** The student uses the appropriate finding tools for a given format.

Terminal Objective 3. The student recognizes that libraries have finding aids appropriate to various subjects.

> **Enabling Objective:** The student uses the appropriate finding tools for a given subject.

Area of Concern: Critical Thinking Skills

General Objective: The student evaluates the usefullness and appropriateness of library materials.

Terminal Objective 1. The student comprehends and analyzes the significance of the components of a bibliographic citation.

> **Enabling Objectives:**
> 1. The student identifies author, title, publisher, abbreviations, journal name, volume number, issue number, pagination, date, bibliography, and illustrations.
> 2. The student explains the significance of the components of a bibliographic citation.

Terminal Objective 2. The student is familiar with scholarly literature.

> **Enabling Objectives:**
> 1. The student compares the value of scholarly and popular literature.
> 2. The student notes the value of abstracts, authors, title, publisher, publication date, descriptors, article length, and tracings.
> 3. The student notices currency, if currency is relevant to the topic.
> 4. The student recognizes the nature of scholarly library materials, including:
>   - Scholarly materials may be refereed or edited.
>   - Scholarly publications may be published by professional and academic organizations.
>   - Scholarly publications have bibliographics or references.
>   - Articles are signed by the authors often with their institutional affiliation given.

Terminal Objective 3. The student understands the process of winnowing a list of bibliographic citations.

> **Enabling Objective:** The student lists citations relevant to a topic.

Terminal Objective 4. The student synthesizes the individual steps of the evaluation process.

> **Enabling Objective:** The student gathers appropriate library materials on a topic.

Area of Concern: Intellectual Access

General Objective: The student knows that library resources use established systems of organization.
Terminal Objective 1.   The student understands that there are certain access points accepted by the research community as the most pertinent for identifying library materials.
  Enabling Objectives:
  1. The student names the author, title, and subject as commonly used access points.
  2. The student realizes that there may be additional access points, including:
     · The student selects additional elements within a citation or abstract as access points.
     · The student identifies other access points that may exist (codes, report numbers, or call numbers, etc.).
  3. The student recognizes that there are controlled vocabularies determined by indexers or catalogers which affect the use of access points.
  4. The student delineates the relationship between broader, related and narrower terms.
Terminal Objective 2.   The student perceives that there are a variety of finding tools whose purpose is to identify library resources using access points.
  Enabling Objectives:
  1. The student uses the appropriate finding tools for a given format.
  2. The student uses the appropriate finding tools for a given subject.
  3. The student acknowledges that no finding tool is fully comprehensive.
Terminal Objective 3.   The student understands how to manipulate access points effectively within established systems of organization.
  Enabling Objectives:
  1. The student browses.
  2. The student describes the aspects of computerized searching, such as Boolean logic, proximity searching, truncation, and keyword searching.
  3. The student is flexible, consulting multiple access tools or changing the direction of the research as appropriate.

Area of Concern: Librarian as Resource

General Objective: The student recognizes the library as a place to seek assistance for information needs.
Terminal Objective 1.   The student views the library staff as a source of assistance.
  Enabling Objectives:
  1. The student locates the Reference Desk.
  2. The student identifies the Reference Desk as the first step in research assistance.
  3. The student requests assistance at the Reference Desk.
Terminal Objective 2.   The student understands that the library staff is comprised of individuals with different areas of expertise.
  Enabling Objective: The student asks for the member of the reference staff qualified to assist in a subject area, when necessary.

Area of Concern: Physical Location

General Objective: The student understands how to locate and retrieve library resources.
Terminal Objective 1.   The student perceives that library materials are grouped in different ways.
  Enabling Objective: The student locates a variety of library resources using a bibliography.
Terminal Objective 2.   The student comprehends that library materials are organized by classification schemes.
Terminal Objective 3.   The student recognizes that most items in the collection have a unique physical address as indicated by its call number.
  Enabling Objectives:
  1. The student locates selected library materials by call numbers.
  2. The student recognizes that there are circumstances when additional material outside the library may be retrieved.

Using the BI Model Statement of Objectives to Develop and Write the Educational Objectives for Locating, Interpreting, and Using Information at the Iowa State University

Rae Haws, Lorna Peterson
Tracy Russell, Diana Shonrock
Iowa State University Library
Ames, Iowa

Iowa State University defines its mission to be "the discovery and dissemination of new knowledge by supporting research, scholarship and student creativity." The University's goal is to "instill in its students the skills essential for their individual development and their useful contribution to society." Achievement of this goal requires that our students know how to find and use information.

Librarians at Iowa State University used the *BI Model Statement* as a basis for creating a document that can be used for information seeking skills curriculum development. In 1988 a "Bibliographic Instruction Work Group" was formed to revise the educational objectives for the Library. The Work Group consisted of ten librarians from various departments of the Library each of whom had some instruction experience. Mechanisms and strategies for implementing these new objectives were left to a follow-up committee and the Library administration. The work group examined the literature and used the *BI Model Statement* along with other information to delineate goals and objectives for future instruction.

The final document delineates goal and objective statements specific to the needs of the students at Iowa State University. Two versions were created; one "short" version is for use within the Library for curriculum development. The other "long" version is meant for distribution to the University community to publicize and clarify new and existing instructional activities.

The objectives contributed to several changes in bibliographic instruction at the Iowa State University Library. Responsibility for all instructional activities was given solely to the newly named Bibliographic Instruction Department rather than dividing them between Reference and Instruction. This includes formal instruction in the form of a credit course required of all freshman, other course related instruction and a series of library use guides. Another major change was the revision of a manual used for the required course which had been in existence since the late 1940's with only minor revisions. Finally, the document resulted in a more organized, clearly articulated plan for bibliographic instruction at Iowa State University.

Iowa State University Library

Educational Objectives

Locating, Interpreting, and Using Information
(Long Version)

Iowa State University defines its mission to be "the discovery and dissemination of new knowledge by supporting research, scholarship and creative activity." The University's goal is to "instill in its students the discernment, intellectual curiosity, knowledge and skills essential for their individual development and their useful contribution to society."[1] The achievement of this goal requires that our students know how to find and use information. Research and scholarship depend upon a knowledge base, a recognition of the need for sufficient evidence before drawing conclusions and the belief that application, analysis and synthesis of information underlie thoughtful judgement.

These concepts should be a part of each student's experience. Teaching the value of information in the scholarly process is the responsibility of the entire Iowa State University faculty. The Library faculty bear particular responsibility for initiating the integration of this value throughout the University curriculum, becoming partners with their classroom colleagues. This process of integration is recognized in a national report as essential to the provision of a quality undergraduate education. College: The Undergraduate Experience in America recommends that for students to become independent self-directed learners "All undergraduates should be introduced carefully to the full range of resources for learning on a campus. They should be given bibliographic instruction and be encouraged to spend at least as much time in the library - using its wide range of resources - as they spend in classes."[2]

The objectives outlined below define what we anticipate all students would achieve by the end of their educational career at Iowa State University. It is our hope that students will learn to use all libraries with ease, confident of their information-seeking skills.

---

[1]"Iowa State University - A Statement of Mission," November 1988.
[2]Ernest L. Boyer, College: The Undergraduate Experience in America, (New York: Harper and Row, 1987), page 165.

Objective A: Students understand what information is and its value in both scholarly and practical processes.

I. Students recognize the need for information when approaching a problem or an issue.

    A. They realize that sufficient evidence is needed before drawing conclusions.
    B. They understand that knowledge is divided into specific areas or disciplines.

        1. They recognize that resources within discipline groups combine information from various sources with original thought, experimental and/or analysis to produce new knowledge.
        2. They are aware that each discipline uses specific methods to communicate information and has a unique structure to its literature.
        3. They are aware that research may involve more than one discipline and more than one method to locate information.

    C. They are aware that there are a variety of information sources, including published, electronic and personal communication.

        1. They are able to identify all the types of resources available including libraries.

II. Students recognize that libraries organize knowledge.

    A. They understand that learning how to use libraries is an integral part of education.
    B. They know that libraries offer many different types of services (e.g., reference, circulation, reserve, photoduplication, special collections, interlibrary loan, collection development).

        1. They are able to identify the appropriate service points to obtain desired information.
        2. They know how to use the library service which satisfies their needs.

    C. They realize that these basic skills are transferable among libraries and can be applied to future learning situations.

III. Students know that libraries provide multiple kinds of information.

    A. They are aware of the various physical formats in which information may be found, such as print, microform, videotape, map, manuscript, electronic database, or computer disc.
    B. They understand the difference between monographs and serials.
    C. They are aware of types of sources available for their research, including primary, secondary, and tertiary.
    D. They are able to distinguish between popular and scholarly materials.

IV. Students understand how to evaluate the sources they select as to accuracy and point of view, including the author's credentials and position, the source's purpose, intended audience, level, timeliness and the relevance for the students' purposes.

    A. They recognize that research and writing result from an individual's creative effort; therefore, credit by means of footnotes and references should be given to the information and interpretation taken from other authors.

Objective B: Students understand standard systems for the organization of information and have the capability to retrieve information from a variety of systems.

I. Students understand general research strategies used to obtain information.

  A. They are able to focus topics, analyze problem statements and seek information.
  B. They are able to ask questions that will obtain needed information.
  C. They are able to use reference materials such as encyclopedias, dictionaries, bibliographies, directories, and handbooks related to their discipline or subject area.

II. Students are aware of and able to use the appropriate sources and library services in order to locate needed information.

  A. They are aware of and able to use the appropriate finding aids in order to locate needed information.

    1. They recognize that various catalogs are used to locate materials.
    2. They are able to interpret the information found in a catalog's bibliographic record.
    3. They know how to select, locate, use and interpret a variety of indexing services in their discipline both in print and electronic forms.

  B. Students are able to physically locate information.

    1. They understand that libraries may group information sources by subject, author, title, format, type of material, publishing agency or special audience.
    2. They recognize that the library's collection encompasses materials in a variety of locations.
    3. They recognize that the same item may be available in various formats which may determine its location in the collection.
    4. They are able to interpret the meaning of library-specific terms (e.g., general collection, tiers, stacks, ranges, current issues).
    5. They know that some materials are shelved in open stacks or on tables while other must be requested at various service desks.
    6. They recognize that materials of a particular subject or discipline are grouped together by classification systems.
    7. They recognize that the unique physical address assigned to each item is a call number and know how to follow a sequence of call numbers to locate a specific item.
    8. They are able to operate equipment required to use various materials.
    9. They recognize that circulation policies vary depending upon the type of material.
    10. They recognize that materials not owned by one library may be obtained from another library.

March 29, 1989

Appendix
Resource Directory Survey

A resource directory of librarians who have had experience with user education programs based on the objectives articulated in the *Model Statement* is housed at the LOEX Clearinghouse.

If you would like to add your name to this directory, please fill in the attached survey and mail to the LOEX Clearinghouse, University Library, Eastern Michigan University, Ypsilanti, MI 48197.

BIS ACCESS TO THE MODEL STATEMENT
OF OBJECTIVES

Survey of Individuals to be listed
in the Resource Directory

Name: _____

Address: _____

_____

_____

_____

Phone: _____

E-mail: _____

FAX #: _____

Indicate your area of experience: (Please Check)

_____   Hands on/writing objectives

_____   Informally helping other write objectives, review documents,
                   making suggestions/editing

_____   Teaching others in a formal setting/giving workshops

_____   Consultant for a fee

_____   Research/publications

Subject areas:

_____   Life Sciences

_____   Physical Sciences

_____   Applied Science and Technology

_____   Fine and Applied Arts

_____   Humanities

_____   Business

_____   Social Sciences

_____   Language/Literature

_____   Law

_____   Medicine

_____   General Education

Levels of courses with which you have experience:

_____   Basic

_____   Advanced

Types of instructional organization:

_____	orientation
_____	Course related
_____	Team Teaching
_____	Integrated
_____	Credit

Areas of Experience:

_____	Online Catalogs
_____	CD-ROMS
_____	Paper indexes
_____	Online Databases
_____	Locally-mounted databases
_____	Networks
_____	Hypermedia
_____	Other

Resources you are willing to share with others:

_____	Copies of objectives for individual classes	Fee?	None ___	Amt ___
_____	Copies of workshop outlines (of workshops teaching how to write objectives)	Fee?	None ___	Amt ___
_____	Copies of class outline/scripts	Fee?	None ___	Amt ___
_____	Talk to someone on the phone	Fee?	None ___	Amt ___
_____	Give a presentation/workshop to other librarians	Fee?	None ___	Amt ___
_____	Review drafts of objectives/give feedback or criticism	Fee?	None ___	Amt ___
_____	Consult	Fee?	None ___	Amt ___

Have you deposited copies of materials with a clearinghouse?

_____	No
_____	Yes

Which one?

_____	LOEX
_____	ERIC
_____	Other (Please list)